LIFE

Film Noir

75 Years of the Greatest Crime Films

Robert Mitchum in
The Night of the Hunter

LIFE

EDITOR AND WRITER J.I. Baker
DIRECTOR OF PHOTOGRAPHY Christina Lieberman
DESIGNER Anne-Michelle Gallero
COPY CHIEF Parlan McGaw
COPY EDITOR Joel Van Liew
PICTURE EDITOR Rachel Hatch
WRITER-REPORTER Amy Lennard Goehner
PHOTO ASSISTANT Christopher Manahan
DIRECTOR OF PHOTOGRAPHY EMERITA
Barbara Baker Burrows

TIME INC. BOOKS

PUBLISHER Margot Schupf
ASSOCIATE PUBLISHER Allison Devlin
VICE PRESIDENT, FINANCE Terri Lombardi
VICE PRESIDENT, MARKETING Jeremy Biloon
EXECUTIVE DIRECTOR, MARKETING SERVICES
Carol Pittard
DIRECTOR, BRAND MARKETING Jean Kennedy
FINANCE DIRECTOR Kevin Harrington
SALES DIRECTOR Christi Crowley
ASSISTANT GENERAL COUNSEL Andrew Goldberg
ASSISTANT DIRECTOR, PRODUCTION
Susan Chodakiewicz
SENIOR MANAGER, CATEGORY MARKETING
Bryan Christian
BRAND MANAGER Katherine Barnet
ASSOCIATE PREPRESS MANAGER
Alex Voznesenskiy
ASSOCIATE MANAGER FOR PROJECT MANAGEMENT
AND PRODUCTION Anna Riego

EDITORIAL DIRECTOR Kostya Kennedy
CREATIVE DIRECTOR Gary Stewart
DIRECTOR OF PHOTOGRAPHY Christina Lieberman
EDITORIAL OPERATIONS DIRECTOR
Jamie Roth Major
SENIOR EDITOR Alyssa Smith
ASSISTANT ART DIRECTOR Anne-Michelle Gallero
COPY CHIEF Rina Bander
ASSISTANT MANAGING EDITOR Gina Scauzillo
ASSISTANT EDITOR Courtney Mifsud

TIME INC. PREMEDIA
Richard K. Prue (Director), Richard Shaffer
(Production), Keith Aurelio, Jen Brown,
Kevin Hart, Rosalie Khan, Patricia Koh, Marco
Lau, Brian Mai, Rudi Papiri, Clara Renauro

SPECIAL THANKS Nicole Fisher, Kristina Jutzi,
Seniqua Koger, Kate Roncinske

CONTENTS

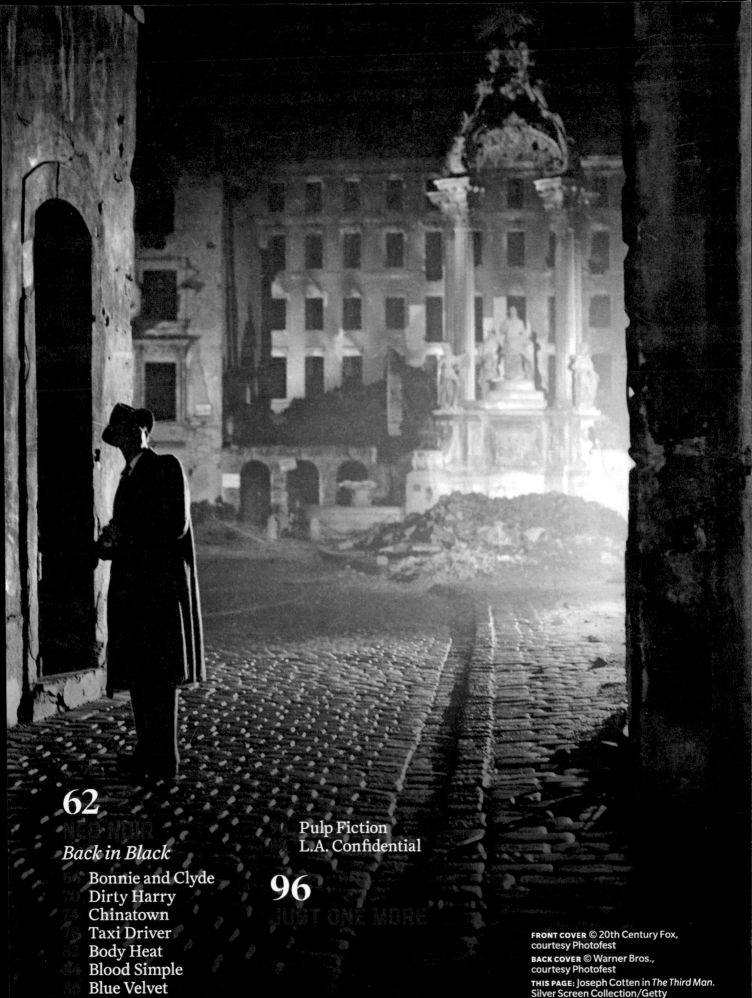

Introduction

BY J.I. BAKER

I n 1933, Joseph Goebbels, the Nazi party's propaganda minister, summoned famed Viennese film director Fritz Lang to his offices, announcing that his 1933 crime film *The Testament of Dr. Mabuse* would be banned. But because of his obvious talent, the Nazis wanted Lang to head the party's film studio. That night, Lang—who had Jewish heritage—fled for Paris.

Just a few years later, Lang was directing the Hollywood crime drama *Fury*—the first of many films he would make for the studios. In the process, he brought (along with Billy Wilder and Alfred Hitchcock, to name just two) the stylized, theatrical influence of German expressionism to American film and merged it with the pulp fiction that had become popular between the wars. (For more on the roots of the genre, see page 8.)

Like jazz, blues, and Broadway musicals, noir became a uniquely American art form by incorporating and transforming foreign influences. And like them, it was often overlooked at first—with its minor stars and low budgets—and was accorded little fanfare. But noir gave Humphrey Bogart and Robert Mitchum career-defining roles; fueled Joan Crawford's middle-age comeback; and set the stage for the work of Martin Scorsese and Quentin Tarantino, among many others. Not least, noir illuminated—well, no, *revealed*— the dark side of the American dream. But despite the bleakness that often characterizes these films, they're somehow always . . . fun.

Seventy-five years after the release of what has been called the first noir, *The Maltese Falcon,* this book revisits 20 of the genre's best. A confession: For every movie reflected here, there are 10 we would kill (no pun intended) to have included. And no doubt there are many you think we unfairly overlooked—but who said life is fair? It surely isn't for the doomed gumshoes and gun molls and gangsters who haunt the perilous world of film noir.

Peter Lorre is a whistling child murderer haunting Berlin's shadowy streets in Viennese director Fritz Lang's 1931 thriller, *M,* which had an enormous influence on film noir. (Lang himself became a well-known practitioner of the form.) "*M* is the ultimate proto-noir," says Jake Hinkson, author of *The Blind Alley,* an exploration of film noir. "It's an unrelenting look at atrocity that also displays a lot of sympathy for the devil. It is both dark and humane in equal measure."

59

CLASSIC N

Barbara Stanwyck, Fred MacMurray, and Edward G. Robinson in *Double Indemnity.*

A Genre Is Born

How German film and pulp fiction inspired a uniquely American art form

he film genre that the French would eventually dub *noir* (meaning "black") was created when the visual tropes of German expressionism (think the stark, angular chiaroscuro and Teutonic angst reflected in such silent classics as *Nosferatu* and *The Cabinet of Dr. Caligari*) were combined with the influence of the pulp and hard-boiled crime fiction that had been popularized in large part by an American magazine called *Black Mask*. Influenced by the terse realism of Ernest Hemingway's fiction, the stories limned a seamy world of fedoras, cheap booze, cheaper bars, guns and gumshoes, double-crossing dames, cynicism, doomed boxers, doomed dreamers, doomed gamblers, and doom itself. Often evocative but mostly pedestrian, the pulp tradition nevertheless spawned three authentic geniuses: Dashiell Hammett, Raymond Chandler, and James M. Cain.

A former operative for the Pinkerton detective agency, Hammett "took murder out of the Venetian vase and dropped it into the alley," according to Chandler. Hammett's prototypical character, the Continental Op, was most famously featured in his first novel, 1929's *Red Harvest*. That same year, the writer introduced his detective Sam Spade, the antihero protagonist of *The Maltese Falcon*, the cinematic adaptation of which has been called the first noir film. (See page 10.)

Of the three writers, Chandler chiefly established the world-weary, cynical voice of the private eye (in his case, Philip Marlowe) that would define so much detective fiction—as well as movie voice-overs. Chandler was also arguably the most poetic stylist of the three, with his masterful use of simile and metaphor. (The director Billy Wilder was particularly fond of this description of an old man: "Out of his ears grew hair long enough to catch a moth.") Chandler's style and unique ear for dialogue were partly why Wilder hired him to co-write the script for 1944's *Double Indemnity* (see page 20), the film that established noir as a major influence on countless future films.

The man who wrote the book that *Double Indemnity* was based on was James M. Cain, who also penned *The Postman Always Rings Twice* and *Mildred Pierce* (see page 28), both of which inspired classic films noirs. Unlike Chandler and Hammett, Cain didn't write from the point of view of a detective. "You can't end a story with the cops getting the killer," Cain once said. "I don't think the law is a very interesting nemesis. I write love stories."

In the end, noir is, in the words of critic Roger Ebert, "the most American film genre, because no society could have created a world so filled with doom, fate, fear, and betrayal, unless it were essentially naive and optimistic."

Above: The vampire Nosferatu in F.W. Murnau's German expressionist classic of the same name. The stark, shadowy imagery of expressionism was an influence on Hollywood noir. (Note the similarity to the image on page 53 from *The Night of the Hunter*.) **Opposite:** The dramatic lighting and dynamic compositions in Orson Welles's 1941 masterpiece, *Citizen Kane*, cast a long shadow (literally) on the burgeoning genre of film noir.

The Maltese Falcon

DIR. JOHN HUSTON

Sure, Humphrey Bogart's portrayal of Sam Spade in John Huston's *The Maltese Falcon* remains the very model of the modern movie detective, but the role was reportedly first offered to tough-guy actor George Raft. And Bogie wasn't the first to step into Spade's gumshoes: Dashiell Hammett's jazz age novel had been made into a film twice before (in 1931, and in 1936 as, of all things, a comedy starring Bette Davis). But in Huston's

A bird in hand is worth . . . well, *a lot*, given the murders and double-crossings that Humphrey Bogart's Sam Spade encounters in this early noir.

From left to right: An unknown actor with Peter Lorre (Joel Cairo) and Humphrey Bogart (Sam Spade) at the Hotel Belvedere in the film that defined the detective genre.

directorial debut, it became the definitive adaptation—and what has been called the first film noir.

Hammett's reworking of two of his 1925 stories from the pulp magazine *Black Mask, The Maltese Falcon* begins when a mysterious, beautiful woman who calls herself Miss Wonderly visits Spade. Though she claims she's looking for her missing sister, it isn't long before the focus shifts to the search for "a black figure of a bird," a.k.a. the titular falcon. After multiple murders, double-crosses, fisticuffs, and a drugging ... well, it's hard to figure out what the heck the mysterious statue actually has to do with anything. But when it comes to noir, a coherent plot is often strictly for the birds.

Unlike the works of noir's two other great pulp progenitors, Raymond Chandler and James M. Cain, *The Maltese Falcon* was (in Huston's hands, at least) faithfully adapted to the screen. Though the director streamlined the action and (due to the censors) trimmed the sex, he kept much of the dialogue— with one significant exception: The famous line referring to the falcon as "the stuff that dreams are made of" was Huston's own (well, paraphrasing Shakespeare). It both joined the cinematic lexicon and reflected the theme of failed quests that would come to define many of Huston's subsequent films.

In addition to kick-starting a lifelong friendship and collaboration between Huston and Bogart, the film featured such marvelous character actors as Sydney Greenstreet; Peter Lorre; and Huston's father, Walter, in roles that were reportedly inspired by people Hammett met in his own career as a Pinkerton detective. Spade, however, "has no original," the writer himself once said. "He is a dream man in the sense that he is what most of the private detectives I worked with would like to have been, and, in their cockier moments, thought they approached."

EVERETT

Shadow of a Doubt

DIR. ALFRED HITCHCOCK

R eportedly inspired by a real-life serial killer who took refuge with his extended family in a small California town, Hitchcock's *Shadow of a Doubt* focuses on the relationship between a young woman nicknamed Charlie (Teresa Wright) and her namesake, the beloved Uncle Charlie (Joseph Cotten). The two are so close, they're almost psychically linked—until Charlie begins to suspect that her uncle is the so-called Merry Widow Murderer, and that he has come to stay with her

© UNIVERSAL PICTURES, COURTESY PHOTOFEST

Uncle Charlie, the Merry Widow Murderer (played by Joseph Cotten), menaces his niece (Teresa Wright) in *Shadow of a Doubt*.

family in Santa Rosa, California, to escape capture back east.

Her growing unease is hardly surprising, given that the genial uncle eventually drops his defenses, revealing a glimpse of the sick monster behind the slick façade. "Do you know the world is a foul sty?" he says to her. "Do you know if you ripped the fronts off houses, you'd find swine?" In this, he echoes the sentiments of serial killers everywhere—both on- and offscreen. ("What sick ridiculous puppets we are," Kevin Spacey's killer says in 1995's *Seven*. "And what gross little stage we dance on.")

Co-written by playwright Thornton Wilder (*Our Town*) and Sally Benson (*Meet Me in St. Louis*)—two eminent chroniclers of small-town Americana—the film was among Hitchcock's favorites, in part because he loved working with Wilder. "In England I'd always had the collaboration of top stars and the finest writers," the master told the French filmmaker François Truffaut, "but in America things were quite different. I was turned down by many stars and by writers who looked down their noses at the genre I work in. That's why it was so gratifying for me to find out that one of America's most eminent playwrights was willing to work with me and, indeed, that he took the whole thing quite seriously."

In the process, the two created something of an anomaly. Though Hitchcock loved stories about wrongly accused men—think Cary Grant in *North by Northwest* or Henry Fonda in, well, *The Wrong Man*—Uncle Charlie's guilt is rarely in question, though it's belied by Cotten's genial blandness. The film is atypical as far as noir goes, too. Much of the genre takes place in urban darkness, but *Shadow of*

a Doubt (despite its title) is awash in wholesome sunlight. But the contrast between the superficially serene surroundings and the dark underbelly represented by Uncle Charlie is what gives the film its

Director Alfred Hitchcock weighs in (top left) and gives pointers to his cast on the Santa Rosa, California, set of *Shadow of a Doubt* (above), shown here in LIFE's exclusive behind-the-scenes story on the making of the film. Though Hitch was used to spending upwards of $100,000 on sets, wartime restrictions dictated that no more than $5,000 could be spent on new materials, forcing the director to shoot on location in New Jersey and Santa Rosa. The cast and crew took over the entire city for four weeks, LIFE wrote, "converting it into a complete motion-picture studio."

GJON MILI/LIFE/THE PICTURE COLLECTION

subversive heft. (Think a portrait of Norman Bates by Norman Rockwell.)

"This is Hitchcock's most wicked vision of America," noir expert and novelist Jake Hinkson tells LIFE. "Go beyond the manicured lawns and the loving family façade, Hitch seems to be telling us, and you'll find neurosis and sociopathy and murder. This is basically *Blue Velvet* 40 years early." (See page 86.) *Blue Velvet*'s director, David Lynch, even paid homage to the surreally dancing figures shown in the Hitchcock film's beginning in the opening of 2001's *Mulholland Drive*.

Though Hitchcock isn't generally associated with noir, he had worked in Berlin early in his career and was deeply influenced by German expressionism, which helped define the genre's look. He also admirered Raymond Chandler, the pulp writer who exerted such an influence on Billy Wilder's *Double Indemnity*, which was released a year after *Shadow of a Doubt*. (See page 20.)

Indeed, Hitch ended up hiring the novelist to co-write his 1951 film, *Strangers on a Train*. Unfortunately, he had even less success with the notoriously difficult man than Billy Wilder did. Never one to hide behind a slick façade, Chandler wrote Hitchcock a scathing letter. "What I cannot understand is your permitting a script which after all had some life and vitality to be reduced to such a flabby mass of clichés, a group of faceless characters," he ranted. "If you wanted something written in skim milk, why on earth did you bother to come to me in the first place?" As to the director himself? Chandler called the Master of Suspense "that fat bastard."

In a series of stroboscopic images created exclusively for LIFE, Alfred Hitchcock shows *Shadow of a Doubt* leading lady Teresa Wright the finer points of being menaced by a serial killer.

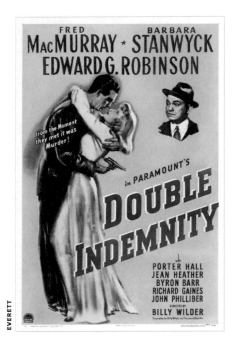

Double Indemnity

DIR. BILLY WILDER

I
n 1925, Ruth Snyder, a New York City housewife, began an affair with Judd Gray, an upstate corset maker. Two years later, after forging an insurance policy, the couple killed her husband, trying to disguise the murder as a botched robbery. But the police quickly saw through the charade—and in 1928, the 32-year-old Snyder was electrocuted at Sing Sing prison. An unprecedented photo of the murderess in the electric chair (see page 34) ran in the *Daily News* under a headline: "DEAD!"

The case was not only a tabloid

Barbara Stanwyck, the avatar of murderous cool, plots with Fred MacMurray in one of *Double Indemnity*'s most famous scenes.

sensation but the inspiration for one of the most influential novels of the 20th century: James M. Cain's *Double Indemnity.* Also known for *The Postman Always Rings Twice* and *Mildred Pierce* (see page 28), Cain was called "the poet of the tabloid murder" by influential critic Edmund Wilson. The novel, in turn, inspired Billy Wilder's adaptation—not only the paradigmatic film noir but "the greatest movie ever made," in the view of Woody Allen.

Starring the usually genial Fred MacMurray as Walter Neff and Barbara Stanwyck as Phyllis Dietrichson—arguably the prototypical femme fatale—the film follows the adulterous couple as they plot to kill her husband for insurance money. Because of its "immoral" elements, the story had been seen as unfilmable. But the wily Wilder found artful ways to avoid censorship—largely through dialogue that relied on metaphor and innuendo. (Consider the often quoted scene between the flirting couple: "There's a speed limit in this state, Mr. Neff. Forty-five miles an hour." "How fast was I going, officer?" "I'd say around 90.")

Much of the credit for this clever repartee goes to Wilder's writing partner, Raymond Chandler, the pulp genius who had been hired when the director's usual collaborator, Charles Brackett, found the project distasteful. The pair's work, though inspired, was contentious: Chandler complained about Wilder's womanizing and Wilder became exasperated by Chandler's drinking. (The director's next film, the noir-inflected *The Lost Weekend,* was about an alcoholic writer and took inspiration from his experience with Chandler.)

The film's success helped push the boundaries of what was acceptable in Hollywood and continues to be an enduring inspiration for directors of all stripes. "I love the tone, the world-view, the cynicism, the wised-up quality of the dialogue," writer-director Lawrence Kasdan tells LIFE, acknowledging the film's influence on his 1981 film, *Body Heat* (see page 82). "It's just one of the most entertaining films ever made."

At left: A rare shot of the film's original ending, in which MacMurray's Neff is sent to the gas chamber, watched (at right) by his boss, played by Edward G. Robinson. Some have suggested the first ending might have worked better than the final version, because it emphasized the bond between the two men, which has been called the film's *real* love story. But director Billy Wilder thought that it was "very anticlimactic." Though the footage has been lost or destroyed, this shot remains. Above: The lovers at the scene of the crime.

Laura

DIR. OTTO PREMINGER

" **I** shall never forget the weekend Laura died," says newspaper columnist Waldo Lydecker (Clifton Webb) at the beginning of the darkly delirious *Laura*. "A silver sun burned through the sky like a huge magnifying glass. It was the hottest Sunday in my recollection. I felt as if I were the only human being left in New York. For Laura's horrible death, I was alone. I ... was the only one who really knew her."

This somewhat overwrought voice-over kicks off what noir expert David Bordwell, Jacques Ledoux Professor of Film Studies, Emeritus, at the University of Wisconsin–Madison, calls "the most hallucinatory noir ever." The film follows hapless New York City

The Mona Lisa of murder: Detective McPherson (Dana Andrews) is haunted by a portrait of the beautiful Laura.

At left: On the set. Above, star Dana Andrews (left) and director Otto Preminger oh-so-casually consult the 1943 novel on which this noir classic was based. Oddly enough, the novel began as a play called *Ring Twice for Laura*. Preminger expressed interest in directing it, but felt it needed a major revise.

The playwright, Vera Caspary, balked—and turned the play into a novel instead. The film reflects a campy, deliberately theatrical quality and the book's florid, mannered style: "The day just past, devoted to shock and misery, had stripped me of sorrow," Caspary wrote in one passage.

detective Mark McPherson (Dana Andrews) as he investigates the alleged shooting death of glamorous advertising executive Laura Hunt (Gene Tierney). While exploring the departed woman's high-society haunts, he begins to fall in love with her—fueled in part by his obsession with her enigmatic portrait.

Directed by Otto Preminger, the film is what critic Roger Ebert called "a tribute to style over sanity." Strictly speaking, not much in the film makes sense—the detective is accompanied throughout by one of the suspects (Lydecker), for instance, and he never reports to the station. But *Laura* is much greater than the sum of its parts, all of which are unified by the classic score (the theme song, "Laura," remains a piano-bar staple).

Then there's the obvious appeal of Tierney. "I've seen the movie 20 times and fall in love with her each time," Otto Penzler, two-time Edgar Award–winning owner of New York's Mysterious Bookshop, tells LIFE. "Pretty much every man watching it does, but Lydecker seems more interested in McPherson."

Sure enough, there is more than a little gay subtext here, fueled in part by Webb's effete performance in his first starring role. But in *Laura*, "every character has a so-called 'perversion,' a wayward or forbidden desire," novelist Megan Abbott tells LIFE: "an older woman for a younger, 'kept' man; a seemingly closeted gay man playing Svengali to a woman in part so he can vicariously experience her relationships with men; and, foremost, a man's necrophiliac love for a dead woman. Desire in *Laura* is never 'straight'—and we are all, it asserts, fundamentally crooked."

Mildred Pierce

DIR. MICHAEL CURTIZ

How do you turn a tearjerker into noir? "Start with a murder, build in complicated flashbacks, and make the striving, suffering heroine a patsy for her second husband, her spoiled daughter, and a real estate man on the make," says noir expert David Bordwell. "Then drench it all in chiaroscuro lighting, and add Joan Crawford's burning eyes and slash-mouth. The result: *Mildred Pierce.*"

A loose adaptation of the 1941 James M. Cain novel, the film follows the titular character, a middle-class housewife and single mother (Joan Crawford) as she struggles to support her entitled elder daughter in Depression-era California. After she reunites with her freeloading ex-lover, "she's expected to take a backseat again," screenwriter and director David Koepp tells LIFE, "as was the case with so many independent American women when the Johnnys came marching home."

The novel's psychological, female-centric approach was atypical for Cain, who was mostly known for the hard-boiled works that spawned such film noir classics as *Double Indemnity* (see page 20) and *The Postman Always Rings Twice.* But in noir, "motherhood is never entirely natural, and female ambition—like all ambition in noir—comes at a heavy price," novelist Megan Abbott tells LIFE. "Foremost, maternal sacrifice is

Steely, sensational Joan Crawford as the redoubtable title character in *Mildred Pierce*— "one of the few noirs about **female ambition, motherhood, and desire," noir novelist Megan Abbott, author of *You Will Know Me,* tells LIFE.**

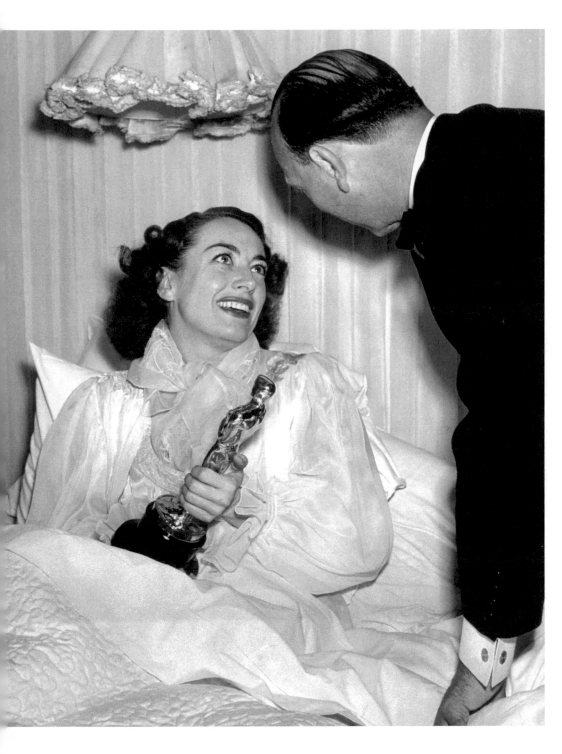

Opposite, top: A beach-house shooting kicks off *Mildred Pierce's* twisty, shifty web of confusion, codependency, and lies. Opposite, bottom: Mildred confronts her devious daughter in the arms of her own paramour in the movie that defined motherly masochism. Left: Reportedly, Crawford faked being sick on Oscar night because she was certain she would lose to the odds-on favorite, Ingrid Bergman in *The Bells of St. Mary's.* When Crawford won, the coveted statuette was delivered by director Michael Curtiz to her in bed, where she *just happened to be* in full makeup—an imaginary invalid who was, in fact, more than ready for her close-up.

not an honorable duty but, in some ways, a perversion." Perhaps as a result of this dynamic, it proved hard to find an actress who wanted to play the middle-aged mom. "I didn't like the story," said actress Ann Sheridan after reading the script. "Mildred was too tough, and the kid was an absolute horror."

When Sheridan, Bette Davis, and Rosalind Russell passed on the role, the 40-something Crawford got the part. It was a risky, if inspired, choice. Only six years earlier, LIFE had called Crawford "the first queen of the movies," but after a string of underwhelming films she had been labeled "box office poison." Even director Michael Curtiz was opposed to her—in part because he didn't like the shoulder pads that had helped define her clotheshorse period at MGM.

But the film became Crawford's comeback, her performance winning a Best Actress Oscar that surprised nearly everyone—not least the actress. "People in Hollywood don't like me," she had said, "and they've never regarded me as a good actress." Not surprising, the film reinvigorated Crawford's career, and the role became as much a part of her enduring image as the shopgirl-on-the-make parts that had first defined her.

After the film's success, Crawford thanked Curtiz with a gift: a pair of custom-made shoulder pads.

TABLOIDS AND FILM NOIR

How photography and journalism inspired the genre

By covering political scandals such as the Teapot Dome bribery incident, and giving ink to poker-game shootings and boozy brawls, the New York *Daily News*—America's first successful tabloid paper—dredged the depths of '20s and '30s culture, replacing staid journalism with lurid photos and a shocking, sleazy sensibility. In the process, it offered narratives tailor-made for the burgeoning world of pulp fiction—and the films noirs that ensued.

Novelist James M. Cain's *Double Indemnity* and *The Postman Always Rings Twice*, for instance, were based on the murderous machinations of Ruth Snyder, who killed her husband with the help of her lover. Dashiell Hammett's *Red Harvest* and David Grubb's *The Night of the Hunter* are among other works that were "ripped from the headlines."

The tabloids also influenced the distinctive look of the films that were inspired by these fictions. In the 1930s, flashbulbs, new cameras, and faster shutter speeds allowed newspaper photographers to ply their trade pretty much anywhere, anytime. The result: a daily documentation of the previously unexplored underbelly of urban existence. Even the *look* of these photos added to their impact: "The lack of naturalness in these pictures was not a shortcoming but a source of their melodramatic power," wrote John Szarkowsi in *Photography Until Now*. "It is as though terrible and exemplary secrets were revealed for an instant by lightning."

Historian Luc Sante has even made a connection between specific photos and subsequent films. "A 1945 picture of a slaying at Tony's Restaurant, with its violent angle, oblique window approach, and mocking use of advertisements, anticipates the blunt force of Anthony Mann's *T-Men* . . . and the jazzy chill of Robert Aldrich's *Kiss Me Deadly*," he wrote, adding that a 1930 shot of

Weegee (near left) was perhaps the first photographer to show crime scenes from the perspective of the onlookers, infusing the depiction of death with distinctly human and emotional elements. Far left: A murder victim outside O Sole Mio Scungilli Bar and Seafood Restaurant in New York City's Little Italy, circa the late 1930s.

Average net paid circulation of THE NEWS, Dec., 1927;
Sunday, 1,357,556
Daily, 1,193,297

DAILY NEWS

EXTRA EDITION

NEW YORK'S PICTURE NEWSPAPER

Copyright, 1928: by News Syndicate Co., Inc. Reg. U. S. Pat. Off.

Entered as 2nd class matter Post Office, New York, N. Y.

Vol. 9. No. 173 56 Pages

New York, Friday, January 13, 1928

2 Cents IN CITY LIMITS 5 CENTS Elsewhere

DEAD!

— Story on page **3**

RUTH SNYDER'S DEATH PICTURED!—This is perhaps the most remarkable exclusive picture in the history of criminology. It shows the actual scene in the Sing Sing death house as the lethal current surged through Ruth Snyder's body at 11:06 last night. Her helmeted head is stiffened in death, her face masked and an electrode strapped to her bare right leg. The autopsy table on which her body was removed is beside her. Judd Gray, mumbling a prayer, followed her down the narrow corridor at 11:14. "Father, forgive them, for they don't know what they are doing?" were Ruth's last words. The picture is the first Sing Sing execution picture and the first of a woman's electrocution. *Story p. 3; other pics. p. 28 and back page.*

(Copyright: 1928: by Pacific and Atlantic photos)

EVERETT (2)

Opposite: The notorious photo of murderess Ruth Snyder being executed in the "death house" in Sing Sing prison on January 12, 1928. According to the New York *Daily News*, it was "perhaps the most remarkable exclusive picture in the history of criminology." At left, top: Actor Ted de Corsia in 1948's documentary-style noir, *The Naked City*, based on Weegee's autobiographical book. At left, bottom: Barry Fitzgerald takes a smoking break against the Manhattan skyline in the same film, shot almost entirely on location.

a homicide at New York's Chinatown People's Theater reflects the look of Howard Hawks's 1932 film *Scarface*.

No photographer was more identified with tabloid journalism than Arthur Fellig, a.k.a. Weegee, who made his name freelancing out of Manhattan's police headquarters. ("Here was the nerve center of the city I knew," he wrote, "and here I would find the pictures I wanted.") With relentlessness and relish, he covered auto accidents, deli holdups, gambling joints, and "jumpers," turning a nation of readers

into rubberneckers even as he imbued ghastly Gotham with a kind of poetry. "Crime was my oyster," Weegee said, "and I liked it."

Weegee's first photography book, 1945's autobiographical *Naked City*, inspired the 1948 noir film *The Naked City*. Reflecting the documentary style that gave many noirs their sense of authenticity, *The Naked City* was shot entirely in New York City and ended with the iconic line "There are eight million stories in the naked city—this has been one of them."

The success of the book and film led to a minor acting career for Weegee. In a self-reflexive Hollywood hall of mirrors, he appeared in a few of the films his work had helped shape: 1949's classic boxing noir, *The Set-Up*, and 1951's forgettable remake of Fritz Lang's proto-noir *M*. Even as the photographer disdained L.A.'s natives as "zombies" ("they drink formaldehyde instead of coffee, and have no sex organs"), he was collecting material for his next book: *Naked Hollywood*, naturally.

EVERETT

Out of the Past

DIR. JACQUES TOURNEUR

I n sleepy Bridgeport, California, an unassuming gas station owner, Jeff Bailey (Robert Mitchum), receives a visit from a man that draws him back into a relationship with a mysterious, murderous woman from his past. And that's only the beginning of this twisted, twisty film's doom-laden romance. "It's extraordinary, my favorite noir," Lawrence Kasdan, the writer-director behind 1981's neo noir *Body Heat*, tells LIFE. "It's a total delight, delicious, and the dialogue is amazing." (When Mitchum's former lover says, "You ought to have killed me for what I did a moment ago," he responds, "There's time.")

Indeed, *Body Heat* was influenced as much by *Out of the Past* as by *Double Indemnity*, Kasdan says, though his film was widely called an unofficial remake of the latter. Like *Double Indemnity*, *Out of the Past* is sharp, laconic, and cynical. It also helped define the genre's distinctive look. According to noir expert Eddie Muller, author of *Dark City*, the film features "the richest chiaroscuro of any noir." But Mitchum, for his part, chalked up the striking cinematography to the film's low budget: "The high-priced actors like Cary Grant back at the studios got all the lights," he said. "So [our set] was lit with cigarettes."

Critic Roger Ebert even called *Out of the Past* "the greatest cigarette-smoking film of all time. The trick . . . is to throw a lot of light into the empty space where the characters are going to exhale. When they do, they produce great white clouds of smoke, which express their moods, their personalities, and their energy levels. There were guns in *Out of the Past*, but the real hostility came when Robert Mitchum and Kirk Douglas smoked at each other."

With the exception of Humphrey Bogart, no star defined the laconic, existential cool—not to mention penchant for nicotine—of the noir antihero more than Robert Mitchum, shown here in a typical pose (albeit atypically without a cigarette). On- and offscreen, these men embodied a cynicism that was both characterized and offset by humor. *Out of the Past*'s script reads, according to Roger Ebert, "like an anthology of one-liners."

Not least among the film's pleasures is watching tyro talents Mitchum and Douglas beginning to establish themselves. "Douglas hadn't really arrived yet, but you can see all the charisma there," says Kasdan. "He was emerging into the persona he was going to inhabit. The same with Mitchum: You can see him coming into his own." Though both stars went on to legendary careers, Mitchum would always be associated with his "humble" noir beginnings. "We called them B pictures," he later said. "We didn't have the money, we didn't have the sets, we didn't have the lights, we didn't have the time. What we did have were some pretty good stories."

At left: Jane Greer as Kathie Moffat, one of noir's greatest femmes fatales. She was reportedly discovered in 1943 by mogul Howard Hughes in the pages of LIFE magazine, where she appeared as a WAC in a war recruitment poster. "Find this girl as soon as possible and sign her up," he said. Above: From left, Paul Valentine, Kirk Douglas, and Mitchum hatch a scheme in a film that's positively filled with them.

The Third Man

DIR. CAROL REED

When the down-on-his-luck American pulp writer Holly Martins (Joseph Cotten) arrives in postwar Vienna at the invitation of his friend Harry Lime (Orson Welles), he discovers that Lime is, in fact, dead—or seems to be. When he learns that Lime had been an unscrupulous racketeer involved in the city's black market, Martins suspects that his friend was murdered … and begins to scarch for the unknown "third man" who was seen carrying Lime's body.

The best British film noir—and one of the best films noirs ever—Carol Reed's *The Third Man*

Orson Welles (far left) as the supposedly deceased Harry Lime in Carol Reed's classic *The Third Man*.

is "genius," David Koepp, the screenwriter behind *Jurassic Park* and the director of *Secret Window*, tells LIFE. Along with *Odd Man Out* (1947) and *The Fallen Idol* (1948)—the two Reed films that immediately preceded it—"*The Third Man* is among the greatest one-two-three punches any director has ever thrown," Koepp adds.

The film was one of three classic collaborations between the director and novelist-screenwriter Graham Greene, who also wrote *The Fallen Idol* and 1959's *Our Man in Havana*. Greene initially wrote *The Third Man* in the form of a novella, which featured a happy ending that Reed

vetoed in the film. "I don't think anything in life ends 'right,'" said Reed, who later won the Best Director Oscar for, of all things, 1968's *Oliver!*

As with so much noir, the film derives a large share of its power from the setting—decaying, bombed-out Vienna, beautifully shot in high-contrast black and white. In Greene's words, Vienna was "simply a city of undignified ruins which turned that February into great glaciers of snow and ice."

The film's distinctive look helped drive the rumor that Welles himself directed the picture. Though this has been discounted, director-critic

Peter Bogdanovich has said that Reed was deeply influenced by Welles's work and that *The Third Man* would be unthinkable without the influence of Welles's 1941 classic, *Citizen Kane*. Welles is, however, widely considered the source of the famous line Lime utters in Vienna's famed Prater amusement park: "In Italy for 30 years under the Borgias, they had warfare, terror, murder, and bloodshed, but they produced Michelangelo, Leonardo da Vinci, and the Renaissance. In Switzerland, they had brotherly love, they had 500 years of democracy and peace—and what did that produce? The cuckoo clock."

Opposite page: Joseph Cotten and Paul Hörbiger watch as Alida Valli places a call. Above: Director Carol Reed (left) and Orson Welles filming in the sewers of postwar Vienna. The film is remarkable on many levels, not least of which is its bleak, stark setting—and the soundtrack's distinctive zither music, played by Anton Karas. (In a happy accident, he was discovered in a restaurant during the production.) At left: Cotten and Welles, who had worked together on Welles's *Citizen Kane* and *The Magnificent Ambersons* and in Welles's Mercury Theatre.

EVERETT

In a Lonely Place

DIR. NICHOLAS RAY

I s the washed-up, volatile screenwriter Dixon Steele stalking and killing women in Hollywood? With Humphrey Bogart as the morally compromised scribe, you can't ever be sure—even as he falls in love with his seductive neighbor (Gloria Grahame, director Nicholas Ray's wife). Will she rescue him … or unearth a dark secret in his past? One of the greatest Hollywood films of the 1950s, *In a Lonely Place* offers many delights—not least "magnificent viewpoint switches worthy of Hitchcock," says noir expert David Bordwell of the University of Wisconsin–Madison.

What's a bleary, beleaguered Bogart doing with a supine broad in bed? Well, he must be *In a Lonely Place*.

© COLUMBIA PICTURES, COURTESY PHOTOFEST

Opposite: Director Nicholas Ray (left) and star Humphrey Bogart on the set of *In a Lonely Place*. In the hands of the two iconoclastic men, the film became a deeply personal meditation on mortality, murder, and the movie business. "In many ways, the film reflects Ray's own self-evisceration," noir novelist Megan Abbott, tells LIFE. Above: Ray's then-wife, Gloria Grahame, takes something less than a joy ride with costar Bogart.

Bogart bought the rights to the source novel by Dorothy B. Hughes in part for its title, which was pretty much all that remained once it reached the screen: Over time, the script increasingly reflected the perspectives of its makers. For both Bogart and Ray, the film was deeply, even painfully, personal. Ray clearly identified with Steele, modeling the character's house after the one he first stayed in after moving to Los Angeles. During the filming, his marriage to Grahame started falling apart—partly because of her offscreen life, which could have been a film noir in itself: She ended up having an affair with Ray's 13-year-old son from a previous marriage—a fact that helped inspire the director's classic 1955 film *Rebel Without a Cause.* (She later married—and divorced—the young man.)

"Achingly romantic and pitch-black, *In a Lonely Place* functions as both love story and an evisceration of a certain kind of predatory masculinity," novelist Megan Abbott, author of *You Will Know Me,* tells LIFE. "But I love it most because it offers Grahame, the quintessential actress of film noir, in her greatest role. Every scene with Grahame and an especially fearless Bogart feels dangerous, beautiful, haunted." Though in some respects *In a Lonely Place* is an anomalous noir—it's not a film of guns and mayhem—it manages, says Otto Penzler, owner of Manhattan's Mysterious Bookshop, to encapsulate the whole genre in a few lines of Steele's: "I was born when she kissed me. I died when she left me. I lived a few weeks while she loved me."

20TH CENTURY FOX/EVERETT

Niagara

DIR. HENRY HATHAWAY

Though sometimes overshadowed by her later turns in musicals, comedies, and "serious" dramas such as *Bus Stop* and *The Misfits,* Marilyn Monroe made an indelible early mark in film noir. She scored her first big break in John Huston's *The Asphalt Jungle* (1950) and later played a homicidal babysitter in *Don't Bother to Knock* and glorified eye candy in noir pioneer Fritz Lang's *Clash by Night* (both 1952).

But true stardom came with 1953's noir *Niagara.* In it, she plays femme fatale Rose Loomis, who is honeymooning with her husband, George (Joseph Cotten), in—naturally—Niagara Falls. After they befriend fellow newlyweds Polly and Ray Cutler, Polly begins to suspect that Rose is having an affair. "Let me tell you something," George says to Polly later. "You're young, you're in love. Well, I'll give you a warning. Don't let it get out of hand, like those falls out there."

As you'd expect, the film makes lavish use of the Niagara Falls location, which critics unabashedly compared to Monroe's body. The *New York Times* reviewer seemed to salivate on the page when he wrote, "They have caught every possible curve both in the intimacy of the boudoir and in equally revealing tight dresses." Unlike other noirs of the time, *Niagara* was filmed in Technicolor, accentuating Monroe's luminous beauty, which was never more apparent—particularly in the magenta dress she wears when she sings "Kiss." Her performance is "noted mostly for her sumptuous visual presence," the novelist Megan Abbott, author of *You Will Know Me,*

tells LIFE, "but it's a knockout role and she takes full advantage of her character's complications and desperation."

Offscreen drama reflected the film's plot: The blonde bombshell was involved at the time with retired baseball star Joe DiMaggio, who was violently jealous when Monroe flaunted her sexuality. ("It's no fun being married to an electric light," he once said.) In the film, George is similarly both attracted and repulsed by his wife's allures. "You smell like a dime store," he says to her. "I know what that means."

The film is "sleazy, gorgeous, and mesmerizing," says Abbott. "Its images, its music, its resort-motel setting all linger in your mind long after you've seen it. It's like a trip you took yourself, one that went very wrong and it's your fault and you know you'll never forget it."

Early in her career, Marilyn Monroe starred in a handful of noirs, but she made a particularly colorful mark in this atypically (for the genre) Technicolor outing.

EVERETT

The Night of the Hunter

DIR. CHARLES LAUGHTON

T he first and only directorial outing from actor Charles Laughton, *The Night of the Hunter* may be "the creepiest noir of all time," Otto Penzler, owner of the Mysterious Bookshop in New York City, tells LIFE. The film famously features Robert Mitchum as Harry Powell, a convict with the words *love* and *hate* tattooed on the fingers of his right and left hands, respectively. "It's the story of good and evil," Harry explains. "You see these fingers, dear hearts? These fingers has veins that run straight to the soul of man."

When Powell learns about a fortune hidden in his condemned cell mate's house, he hatches a

Robert Mitchum reveals the deeply sinister side of his trademark cool to *The Night of the Hunter*'s embattled innocents.

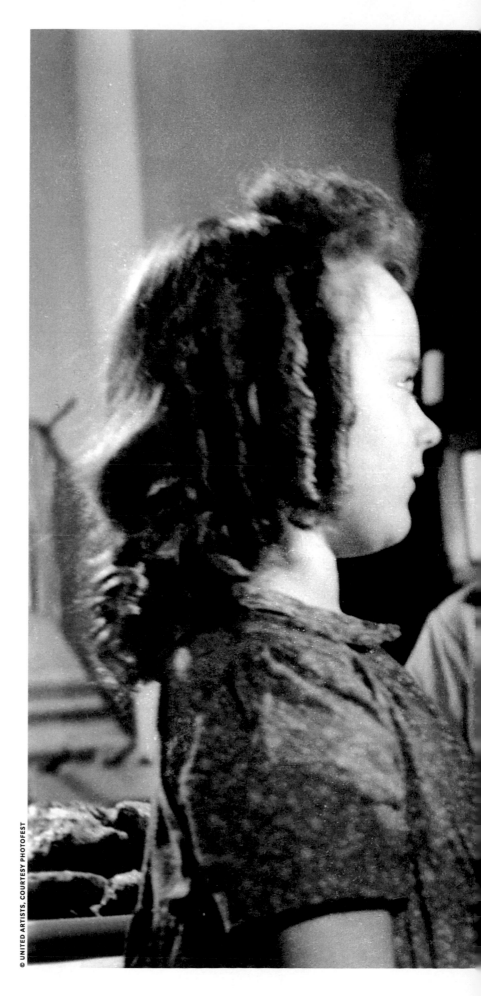

© UNITED ARTISTS, COURTESY PHOTOFEST

plan. Once released from prison, determined to possess the money, he seduces the man's widow (Shelley Winters). When she dies, he pursues her two children in a mythic trip down a dark river.

Set in Depression-era West Virginia, *The Night of the Hunter* embodies the Southern gothic tradition, "redolent of strange sex, bad booze, old-time religion, and the collective regional memory of defeat," according to critic Terrence Rafferty. But the physical location is almost beside the point, since the film seems to rise from the deep wellsprings of the unconscious, the liminal place where nightmares breed. In fact, it has often been called a horror film. (The harrowing scene in which Mitchum shouts at the children from the top of the stairs has been endlessly imitated but never bettered.)

Laughton was clearly inspired by film pioneer D.W. Griffith—"the master of heightened, poetic melodrama," Rafferty continued. (Griffith regular Lillian Gish even has a pivotal role.) "It's as if Laughton had resolved to recover something the movies had lost, some secret, long-forgotten cache of letters from ancestors—the scripture of the art's early magic."

The film is defiantly expression-istic, reflecting the noir genre's roots. ("The town looks as artificial as a Christmas card scene," critic Roger Ebert wrote.) And its dark fairy-tale quality brings to mind the likes of "Hansel and Gretel" as much as *Out of the Past* or *Double Indemnity*. "It's really a nightmarish sort of Mother Goose tale we are telling," Laughton said. "We tried to surround the children with creatures they might have observed, and that might have seemed part of a dream."

Below: Screen pioneer Lillian Gish gets her gun in *The Night of the Hunter*, a poetic, dreamlike film that has more in common with French poet and filmmaker Jean Cocteau's *Beauty and the Beast* than, say, *Double Indemnity*. At right: Mitchum pursues the kids in a scene reflecting the look of F.W. Murnau's *Nosferatu*. (Compare it to the image on page 8.)

Orson Welles's corrupt police captain (right) confers with a Mexican crime boss (Akim Tamiroff) in the gleefully excessive *Touch of Evil*.

Touch of Evil

DIR. ORSON WELLES

Quite possibly no director had a greater impact on film noir than the erratic genius Orson Welles. The distinctive high-contrast lighting of his first film, 1941's classic *Citizen Kane*, helped define the genre's look, and Welles later directed such full-blown noirs as *Journey into Fear* (1943) and *The Lady from Shanghai* (1947). He also had a pivotal part in 1949's *The Third Man* (see page 40). But his greatest work in the tradition is arguably 1958's *Touch of Evil*.

Stark and delirious, the gothic thriller begins with a car bombing along the U.S.–Mexican border, which attracts the attention of Mike Vargas (Charlton Heston), a Mexican drug-enforcement official, and Hank Quinlan (Welles), a corrupt police captain. "It's the sleaziest noir ride

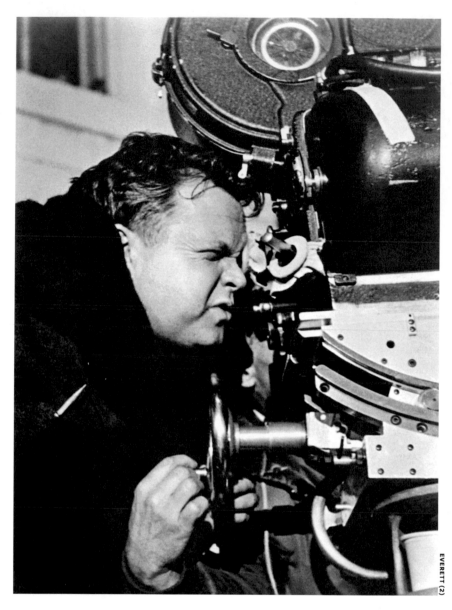

ever," noir expert and novelist Jake Hinkson tells LIFE. "Welles wanted to push noir as far as it could go, and he comes pretty close to pushing it to the edge of insanity." Called "film noir's epitaph" by writer-director-critic Paul Schrader (screenwriter of *Taxi Driver*), the film basically marked the end of the genre's classic era.

But Universal Studios hated the film and cut it to 93 minutes. That was the only version available until 1976, when the studio released a longer version that had been found in the archives. Though Welles was alive at the time, he was never consulted about the rerelease, and it wasn't until 1998 that the extended cut was restored to what he might have intended, following

the meticulous directions he had outlined in a memo to Universal. "Seeing it pure was wonderful," said the film's costar Janet Leigh, who cried during a screening. "I was so thrilled that this genius is going to have a chance to show itself again."

"Your future is all used up," the fortune-teller Tana (Marlene Dietrich) tells Hank toward the end of the film. *Touch of Evil* was Welles's last Hollywood effort as a director, though he continued to act there. Considered "unbankable" stateside, he decamped to Europe to write and direct his own films. Though he made successful adaptations of Shakespeare (*Othello* and the acclaimed *Chimes at Midnight*), financing was a perennial struggle and many projects remained

unfinished. He took commercial work, using his gravitas and arresting baritone to sell supermarket wine and frozen food. He was also a frequent talk-show guest. Hours after taping his last appearance—on *The Merv Griffin Show* in 1985—Welles died, hunched over a typewriter, his future all used up.

At left: Welles behind the camera on the set of his Hollywood swan song.

Above: the film's strip club, run by a character played, in a brief cameo, by Zsa Zsa Gabor.

OFFSCREEN NOIR

Meet the actors whose lives were as dark as their films

Drug busts, drunken fisticuffs, illicit sex, murder: the ingredients of classic film noir, right? Well, yes, but they were also events in the lives of certain noir actors, proving that the genre offered a more accurate reflection of Hollywood reality than such cinematic cream puffs as *Father of the Bride* and *Harvey*. Thanks to the studio system's controlling image factory and a malleable press, stars' lives were publicly idealized. But the celebrities themselves wrestled with the same foibles and faults that beset the rest of us—and then some.

"Well, this is the bitter end of everything—my career, my home, my marriage," actor Robert Mitchum said in 1948 after being busted for smoking marijuana in Los Angeles's Laurel Canyon. But the public didn't seem to mind—maybe because the arrest simply reinforced Mitchum's bad-boy image, honed in the likes of the 1947 noir classic *Out of the Past* (see page 36). The Mitchum movie that followed, *Rachel and the Stranger*, was a hit, and his career continued—cannabis be damned.

In 1950, Humphrey Bogart bought the rights to noir novelist Dorothy B. Hughes's *In a Lonely Place*, which he and director Nicholas Ray turned into a film that reflected their own disordered lives rather than the book's plot. (See page 44.) Like the movie's putatively homicidal hero, Bogart was a cynical heavy drinker, prone to alcoholic pugilism that he did very little to hide.

"Sometimes, when [Bogart] and his wife, a plump blonde whom he calls 'Sluggy,' are in the midst of one of the brawls which they frequently engage in before their friends, she will suddenly pick up her highball and heave it at him," LIFE wrote in 1944. "He never troubles himself to duck, but sits calmly in his chair while the glass whizzes by, uncomfortably close to his valuable face. As it shatters against the wall behind him, he shakes his close-cropped head and announces, 'I live dangerously. I'm colorful. But Sluggy's crazy about me.'"

In the 1950s, as Bogart was dying from esophageal cancer brought on by decades of heavy smoking and drinking, he claimed to regret a single bad decision: "I should never have switched," he said, "from scotch to martinis."

Opposite: Robert Mitchum jailed after his pot bust. Left: Humphrey Bogart after his 1949 summons for simple assault.

ULLSTEIN BILD/GETTY

Female stars were often just as reckless. *Mildred Pierce*'s Joan Crawford was promiscuous, tyrannical, and allegedly sometimes violent; and Bogart's *In a Lonely Place* costar, Gloria Grahame, bedded the 13-year-old son of her husband, the film's director. But no noir actress was more notorious than the so-called Sweater Girl, Lana Turner, who starred as the murderous wife in the 1946 adaptation of James M. Cain's noir *The Postman Always Rings Twice*.

Married eight times (to seven husbands), Turner had many lovers in addition to her connubial couplings—the most infamous being the mob-connected Johnny Stompanato. Their violent partnership was severed on April 4, 1958. "He grabbed me by the arms," Turner later said, "and started shaking me and cursing me very badly, and saying . . . that if he said jump, I would jump; if he said hop, I would hop, and I would have to do anything and everything he told me or he'd cut my

face or cripple me. And if . . . when it went beyond that, he would kill me and my daughter and my mother."

He did not have the chance. When the fighting that night became so extreme that Cheryl Crane, Turner's daughter, feared for her mother's life, she stabbed the mobster with a butcher knife. The day after the murder was ruled "justifiable homicide," the *Los Angeles Times* called Turner a hedonist who lacked moral sensitivity. "Cheryl isn't the juvenile delinquent," the paper said. "Lana is."

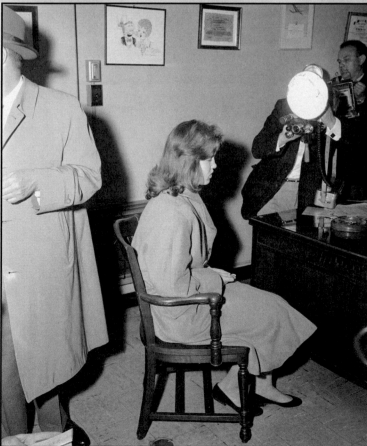

Opposite: Police investigate the stabbing murder of Lana Turner's lover, Johnny Stompanato, by her daughter, Cheryl Crane. Above: Turner giving what has been called "the most important performance of her life" at the coroner's inquest. At left: Crane, just before being booked at the Los Angeles County Juvenile Hall.

NEO NOIR

1967 – 1997

The voyeuristic tendencies of Jeffrey Beaumont (Kyle MacLachlan) get the better of him in *Blue Velvet*.

Back in Black

How the pulp traditions of the past inspired a bold new cinematic future

n 1958, the failure of *Touch of Evil* brought Orson Welles's Hollywood directing career to an end, taking film noir into the cinematic dustbin along with it. Angling to compete with television, movie houses were suddenly filled with Cinerama and Cinemascope spectacles, which were inimical to the paranoid, claustrophobi␣␣ibe that had defined noir. (There were exceptions, of course—Hitchcock's *Vertigo* and *Rear Window* come to mind—but they mostly proved the rule.)

Noir was hardly dead, though. While audiences flocked to the likes of *The Sound of Music*, American living rooms were alive with the sound of *Dragnet*'s narrator intoning: "The story you are about to see is true. The names have been changed to protect the innocent." Beginning in the late '50s, noir resurfaced in such gritty, ostensibly realistic TV shows as the revamped *Dragnet*, *Peter Gunn*, and *The Fugitive*.

However, the genre began making a cinematic comeback in the late '60s, arguably spurred by *Bonnie and Clyde*, which broke all the mainstream rules with its dry mix of comedy and violence, the apotheosis of which was its grisly, unprecedentedly realistic climactic killing of the pair. (The film was something of an updating of the 1950 noir classic *Gun Crazy*.)

But the seminal neo noir, a breakthrough film that almost single-handedly revitalized the genre even as it faithfully paid tribute to its progenitors, was Roman Polanski's *Chinatown* (1974). Often called the greatest crime movie ever made (and Robert Towne's script the greatest screenplay ever written), *Chinatown* harked back to the fiction of Raymond Chandler while proving that—as with so many films in the decades that followed—everything old could be new again.

Other influences on neo noir included, of course, the Vietnam War, the rise of international terrorism, Wall Street corruption, and AIDS. And women's rights advocates were often seen as, well, "feminists fatales" by so-called red-blooded American males who were not keen to change their ways. In short, the '70s and '80s created an environment in which an antihero like Clint Eastwood's morally questionable Dirty Harry could tell punks to make his day—and Robert De Niro as Travis Bickle, the taxi driver from hell, could ask, "You talkin' to *me*?"

Above: Two generations of noir genius. From left to right, director Roman Polanski, director-actor John Huston, and star Jack Nicholson behind the scenes of the revolutionary *Chinatown*. Huston had directed *The Maltese Falcon* (see page 10), the original detective film noir.

Bonnie and Clyde

DIR. ARTHUR PENN

Just before dawn on May 23, 1934, the notorious criminal Clyde Barrow and his companion, Bonnie Parker, were ambushed and shot to death by police officers while driving a stolen car near Sailes, Louisiana. It was the suitably dramatic end to an extended crime spree: For nearly two years, the couple had roamed Texas and Oklahoma, committing 13 murders and multiple robberies. In the process, they gained notoriety as a Depression-era Robin Hood and his murderous Maid Marian.

Their lurid legend was further burnished with the ground-breaking *Bonnie and Clyde*, starring Warren Beatty and Faye Dunaway. Anticipating other genre reinventions that later fueled the comparatively toothless *Raiders of the Lost Ark* and *Star Wars*, *Bonnie and Clyde* was a contemporary spin

The terrible twosome (Faye Dunaway and Warren Beatty) use a tire for target practice, opposite. Bottom: Beatty didn't direct *Bonnie and Clyde*, but he belied his pretty-boy status by exerting a committed, visionary, and almost obsessive control on the set. "It is all detail, detail, detail," he once said. "That's where the stamina comes in." The relentless lothario showed plenty of stamina offscreen, too.

JERRY TAVIN/EVERETT

on '30s gangster movies. To this bad-boy bedrock the filmmakers added the influence of the French new wave, exemplified by the work of François Truffaut and Jean-Luc Godard, both of whom had been approached to direct.

Prefiguring the work of Quentin Tarantino by 25 years, the film mixed farce and eroticism with unprecedented violence—particularly in the final ambush, in which Clyde and Bonnie are riddled with bullets in a scene that left nothing to the imagination. Partly as a result, the film's studio, Warner Bros., was leery of the film—as were many critics. (The *New York Times* damned it as both "strangely antique,

sentimental claptrap" and "reddened with blotches of violence of the most grisly sort.")

But audiences embraced the antiheroic antics. Released at a time marked by both the acid-soaked utopian Summer of Love and mass protests against the Vietnam War, the film became a counterculture touchstone. Just as the murderous couple had become Depression-era folk heroes, so their cinematic counterparts spoke to the youth of the antiauthoritarian 1960s. In the film, for instance, Bonnie reads a poem: "If a policeman is killed in Dallas / and they have no clue to guide / if they can't find a fiend / they just wipe their slate clean / and hang it on Bonnie and Clyde."

Below: Buck Barrow, Clyde Barrow, and Bonnie Parker (Gene Hackman, Beatty, and Dunaway), having just made a withdrawal at the bank. In actuality, Bonnie and Clyde robbed relatively few banks, stealing instead from gas stations and grocery stores, their haul often only five or 10 bucks. Opposite: Dunaway and Beatty are the height of criminal chic. The real-life Bonnie and Clyde were far less photogenic, but they did pose for photos that went public.

Dirty Harry

DIR. DON SIEGEL

Of all the cinematic catchphrases that have become part of the American lexicon, none is more indelible than "Go ahead, make my day," the vigilante cop Harry Callahan's feral challenge to the bad guys in the *Dirty Harry* quintet. The first—and finest—film in the series follows San Francisco homicide detective Callahan (Clint Eastwood), armed with his famed .44 Magnum, as he stalks the Scorpio killer. (The film's fey psychopath was loosely modeled on the real-life Zodiac killer, who terrorized California's Bay Area in the late '60s and early '70s.)

Released in the wake of political assassinations and increasing outrage at the Vietnam War, *Dirty Harry* captured the national zeitgeist and came as a salutary shock to the system, fueling controversy surrounding such issues as police brutality and victims' rights. "It would be hard to argue [that] the film (like Harry) is not racist, homophobic, and devoid of a genuine respect for what most of us consider constitutional liberties," according to Charles Silver, curator of the Museum of Modern Art's department of film. Indeed, outside the 44th Academy Awards, protestors carried placards reading "Dirty Harry Is a Rotten Pig."

Critics were divided, too, with the *New Yorker*'s Pauline Kael calling it "a deeply immoral movie." But *Dirty Harry* eventually came to be seen as a great American film. In 2012, it became part of the prestigious National Film Registry. And Harry—the archetypal antihero of the '70s—became a career-defining role for Eastwood, who until then had been mostly known as the Man with No Name in Sergio Leone's spaghetti Westerns.

Though Eastwood was not the first choice for the role, which had been offered to the aging likes of John Wayne and Frank Sinatra, he is now inseparable from the image of the anarchic avenger. Once, when speaking to a film class, Eastwood launched into Harry's signature "Do you feel lucky?" speech "like it was yesterday," he said. "Everybody loved it. I've never said anything to an audience that's pleased them more. Everybody was going, 'Yeah! Yeah!' I could have taken that audience to war."

Opposite page: Clint Eastwood as rule-breaking detective Harry Callahan takes aim in *Dirty Harry.* **At left: Eastwood with director Don Siegel in front of a marquee advertising** *Play Misty for Me,* **the Eastwood-helmed film that was released during** *Dirty Harry's* **filming. Siegel had made his mark in a number of seminal early noirs, including** *Riot in Cell Block 11* **(1954) and** *The Killers* **(1964).**

Above: Harry on the prowl. Left: Eastwood with his son Kyle. Opposite: The cheerful star is shown after filming a brutal beating scene.

Chinatown

DIR. ROMAN POLANSKI

f Truman Capote hadn't penned a disastrous screenplay for *The Great Gatsby* in the early '70s, *Chinatown* might never have been made. Trying to salvage the project, producer Robert Evans asked script doctor Robert Towne to rewrite the screenplay. But Towne didn't relish the idea of taking on F. Scott Fitzgerald. Instead, he told Evans about a film that he was writing for Jack Nicholson. It was, Towne said, the story of "how L.A. became a boomtown: incest and water."

Towne meant the so-called rape of the Owens Valley, from which water was diverted to the dry Los Angeles desert by means of an aqueduct the city constructed in the early 1900s. Directed by Roman Polanski, *Chinatown* uses this historical event to fuel a labyrinthine plot that can't be effectively summarized here. So let's just say that it begins in 1937 Los Angeles when a mystery woman (Diane Ladd) asks J.J. Gittes (Nicholson), a sleazy detective straight out of pulp noir, to spy on her husband. Naturally, she thinks he's cheating on her. The visit leads Gittes into a web of deception, perversion, and the mystery surrounding Los Angeles's water supply.

In the hands of Polanski, the film took on a far darker cast than Towne had intended. The director wanted *Chinatown* to be "special, not just another thriller where the good guys triumph in the final reel."

The sinister sensibility the director brought to nearly all his films was nothing if not personal. A Holocaust survivor, he had endured the murder of his pregnant wife, Sharon Tate, at the hands of the Manson family just a few years before. And his personal life remained controversial. In 1977, he was arrested for drugging and raping a 13-year-old girl in Nicholson's hot tub, and he fled the U.S. before final sentencing.

Chinatown celebrated its 40th anniversary in 2014, yet it probably would not be made in contemporary Hollywood, according to Towne. In the '70s, "a series of shared beliefs … focusing on what was wrong with the country, created a sense of communion between filmmakers and filmgoers," he wrote. "We share no such beliefs today … It's difficult to lie credibly without belief in the truth." *Chinatown* remains the most iconic neo noir ever and the one that reintroduced the genre to modern audiences. "It's film noir as the Great American Movie," novelist Jake Hinkson tells LIFE. "It really doesn't get any better—any darker, any truer, any sadder—than this."

Faye Dunaway (as Evelyn Mulwray) tends to the slashed schnoz of Jack Nicholson (J.J. Gittes) while contemplating, it seems, more intimate ministrations.

PARAMOUNT/KOBAL/ART RESOURCE, NY

Opposite: Gittes offers Evelyn an immodest proposal. Above: Evelyn is up in arms. At right: Gittes in front of the sign that reflects *Chinatown*'s shady water politics, based on what was known as the rape of the Owens Valley and motivated, of course, by greed. At one point, addressing John Huston as millionaire Noah Cross, Gittes asks, "How much better can you eat? What can you buy that you can't already afford?" Cross's reply: "The future." Diverting the water from the valley did turn Los Angeles from a desert to a boomtown, but nature always wins in the end: The City of Angels faces an enduring drought.

Taxi Driver

DIR. MARTIN SCORSESE

"**S**omebody's going to get me one of these days," the controversial politician George Wallace once told the *Detroit News*. "I can just see a little guy out there that nobody's paying any attention to. He reaches into his pocket and out comes the little gun." On May 15, 1972, Wallace's premonition came true when a "little guy" named Arthur Bremer fired five times at the politician during a Maryland campaign stop, paralyzing Wallace for life.

The man and the event eventually inspired screenwriter Paul Schrader, who saw in Bremer a mirror of his own frustration and fury. ("Travis Bickle is me," he once said. "At the time I wrote [*Taxi Driver*], I was in a rather low and bad place.") But unlike the assassin, Schrader parlayed his existential angst into a script "to exorcise the evil I felt within me."

The work caught the attention of Martin Scorsese, ultimately becoming the director's neo noir classic *Taxi Driver*, which follows Travis Bickle (Robert De Niro), a disturbed Vietnam vet, as he prowls a degenerate New York City in his cab.

Robert De Niro as Travis Bickle, the titular taxi driver, cruising Manhattan's mean streets.

EVERETT

The self-appointed savior of a child prostitute (Jodie Foster), Bickle ends up trying to assassinate a politician. The film was very much of its time: In 1976 Manhattan was edgy and dangerous. (That year, the *New York Times* printed a list of 101 things to love about New York City, including "People who haven't left yet.")

Unnervingly, the film's dynamics played themselves out in real life in 1981, when John Hinckley Jr. tried to get Foster's attention by attempting to assassinate then-president Ronald Reagan. Schrader and Scorsese were even interviewed by FBI agents, who wanted to know if Hinckley had contacted them. Though he didn't respond

truthfully at the time, Schrader later admitted that he had received letters (which he ignored) from "this kid in Colorado who wanted to know how he could meet Jodie Foster."

Recently Scorsese has said that he would have made the film in 3-D if he could have. Imagine *Taxi Driver* at IMAX theaters alongside *Finding Dory*.

Above: De Niro (left) and director Martin Scorsese on the set. At right: Jodie Foster as the child prostitute whom Bickle tries to save. Fueled by screenwriter Paul Schrader's feelings

of despair, anger, and stasis, the film also reflected the life of Arthur Bremer, who attempted to assassinate Alabama governor George Wallace in 1972. "I want something to happen,"

Bremer wrote in his infamous diaries. "I want a big shot & not a little fat noise . . . tired of writing about . . . what I failed to do again and again." Later, the film infamously inspired John

Hinckley Jr.'s 1981 attempted assassination of President Ronald Reagan. "I love you forever," Hinckley wrote to Foster in an unmailed letter, just before he made his move.

The simultaneously sinister and sultry seduction typical of noir is revisited and eroticized in Lawrence Kasdan's breakthrough neo noir, with William Hurt and a then-unknown Kathleen Turner. Opposite: Turner in histrionic mode.

LADD COMPANY/WARNER BROS./KOBAL/ART RESOURCE, NY

Body Heat

DIR. LAWRENCE KASDAN

I n 1944's classic noir *Double Indemnity,* writer-director Billy Wilder outmaneuvered the Hollywood censors through clever elusiveness and sly suggestion: The film worked in part because of what *wasn't* said or shown. (See page 20.) Some four decades later, writer-director Lawrence Kasdan's update, *Body Heat,* brilliantly revels in things that Wilder could only hint at ... chief among them, of course, sex.

The prototype for a series of erotic thrillers that followed its success, *Body Heat* revolves around an adulterous affair between lawyer Ned Racine (William Hurt) and Matty Walker (Kathleen Turner). Not surprisingly, they conspire to kill her husband, with plenty of twists and turns (and did we mention sex?) along the way—along with dialogue straight out of classic noir. "You're not too smart, are you?" Matty says. "I like that in a man."

This kind of language was part of what inspired Kasdan. Though he was a successful screenwriter hot off *The Empire Strikes Back* and *Raiders of the Lost Ark,* he had never directed a film. "I was worried that I would never get another chance, so I wanted to try as many things as I could," he tells LIFE. "Noir gives you enormous license with the camera, license for stylized dialogue. I wanted to do a movie that wasn't naturalistic and to have a lot of fun with it."

Even though the film has been widely called an unofficial remake of *Double Indemnity,* Kasdan says that 1947's *Out of the Past* was possibly an even greater influence. (See page 36.) "It has a very high level of wit and worldliness to it," he says of *Out of the Past.* "It's funny and sly and wry and twisted and wonderful."

Though a noir in color seems a contradiction in terms, *Body Heat* successfully translates the chiaroscuro of its predecessors by accentuating the intense orange glow of the sultry Florida weather. There's plenty of sweaty skin glistening in the southern sun on display, though the film was shot during one of the coldest Florida summers on record. "Few movies have done a better job of evoking the weather," critic Roger Ebert wrote.

Kasdan's follow-up, *The Big Chill,* which also stars Hurt, would seem leagues away from his debut, but the director sees the films as intimately connected. "Ned Racine wants to hit it big without doing the work, without doing what's necessary— something I felt was rife among my contemporaries," he says, "and that's so much of what informs *The Big Chill.* So *Body Heat* was very much about that for me: What happens when a guy who has personal charm and has done well with women but isn't effective in the world runs into someone who's effective in the world?"

Blood Simple

DIR. COEN BROTHERS

This damned burg's getting me," says the Continental Op, the narrator of *Red Harvest*, the 1929 novel by seminal hard-boiled author Dashiell Hammett. "If I don't get away soon I'll be going blood-simple like the natives. There's been what? A dozen and a half murders since I've been here."

Though Joel and Ethan Coen's debut film, 1984's *Blood Simple,* took its title from this quote, its true literary progenitor was pulp author James M. Cain. "We especially liked *The Postman Always Rings Twice, Double Indemnity, Mildred Pierce,* and *Career in C Major,*" Joel has said of the literary building blocks of film noir. (See pages 20 and 28.) "We liked the hard-boiled style, and we wanted to write a James M. Cain story and put it into a modern context."

Three years after Lawrence Kasdan's *Body Heat* redefined film noir for '80s audiences, the low-budget *Blood Simple* offered a bleak, relentless story about a Texas bar owner, Julian Marty (Dan Hedaya), who hires a private investigator (M. Emmet Walsh) to kill his cheating wife (Frances McDormand)—only to be double-crossed. (Naturally.)

The Kasdan and Coen films were connected more than just thematically, though: *Blood Simple* made a number of visual nods to *Body Heat,* according to the director of photography, Barry Sonnenfeld, whose creative camera work helped define the film. (He later directed *Men in Black.*)

Together, the two movies helped inspire a string of steamy thrillers that followed. (Think 1992's sleazy, cheesy *Basic Instinct,* starring Michael Douglas, and Sharon Stone's private parts.)

The protean Coens went on to a wildly varied career that encompassed a variety of genres, but they've frequently returned to noir in such films as *Fargo, The Big Lebowski, No Country for Old Men,* and *The Man Who Wasn't There.* (The latter was even more explicitly influenced by Cain than *Blood Simple* was.) The Coen's debut remains a critical favorite, though, and is the only one of their films that has been remade: The great Chinese director Zhang Yimou called his 2010 version *A Woman, a Gun, and a Noodle Shop,* a.k.a. *A Simple Noodle Story.*

Along with *Body Heat*, the Coen brothers' debut, *Blood Simple*, brought noir kicking and screaming (and killing and seducing) into the '80s, with Frances McDormand as Abby (opposite, and with Dan Hedaya as Julian Marty above).

Blue Velvet

DIR. DAVID LYNCH

One of the greatest American films of the 1980s—if not of all time—kicks into gear when college student Jeffrey Beaumont (Kyle MacLachlan) finds a severed ear in a field in the fictitious town of Lumberton, North Carolina. "It had to be an ear because it's an opening," writer-director David Lynch has said of his masterpiece, *Blue Velvet*. "An ear is wide and, as it narrows, you can go down into it. And it goes somewhere vast."

When Jeffrey tries to solve the auricular mystery by breaking into the apartment of saloon singer Dorothy Vallens (Isabella Rossellini), he sparks the wrath of psychosexual sadist Frank Booth (a blisteringly brilliant Dennis Hopper). "I had always wanted to sneak into a girl's room to watch her at night," Lynch has said of the film's inspiration. "Maybe, at one point or another, I would see something that would be a clue to a murder mystery."

A defining neo noir, *Blue Velvet* clearly has its roots in classic noir, and owes a debt to both *Rear Window* and *Sunset Boulevard*, among others. "*Rear Window* is one

"The Blue Lady," Dorothy Vallens (Isabella Rossellini), in David Lynch's visionary *Blue Velvet*.

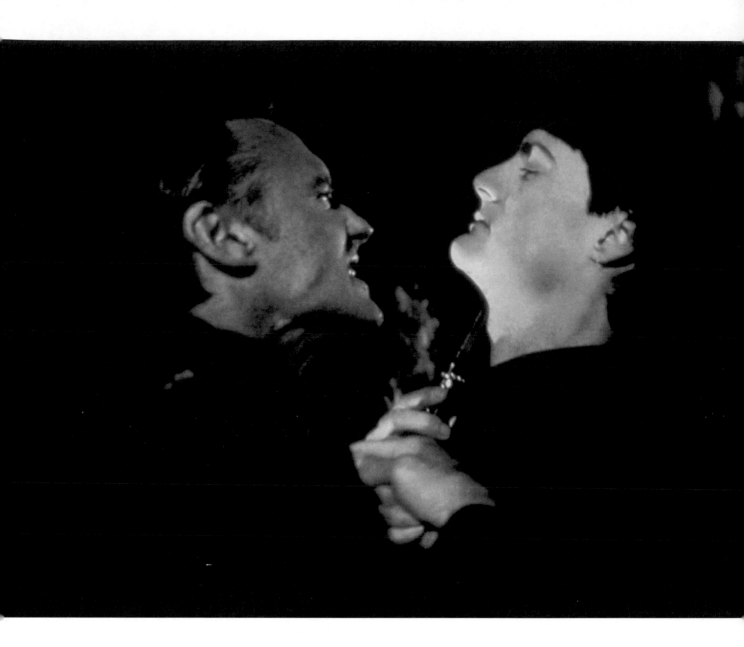

of my favorite movies," the director has said, "because it's got such a mood, and even though I know exactly what happens next, I enjoy to be in that room and feel that time. It's almost like I could smell it."

Though often erratic, Lynch's subsequent work continued to reflect his noir inspirations, with *Blue Velvet* becoming the template for his 1990s cult TV series, *Twin Peaks*. And *Sunset Boulevard* was a prominent influence on 2001's *Mulholland Drive*, the director's dark valentine to Hollywood. But Lynch never equaled the combination of perversion and exhilaration that defined *Blue Velvet*. As of 2016, he hadn't directed a feature film in a decade.

Thirty years after *Blue Velvet*'s release, it's not easy to understand just how raw and shocking its surreal sexuality and violence were at the time. The singer Roy Orbison—whose song "In Dreams" is prominently featured in the film—has said that viewing it reminded him of seeing Elvis Presley for the first time in 1955. "He came out and spat out a piece of gum," the singer said. "I can't overemphasize how shocking he looked and seemed that night . . . It affected me exactly the same way as when I first saw that David Lynch film. I just didn't know what to make of it. There was just no reference point in the culture to compare it."

Above: Dennis Hopper as Frank Booth menaces Kyle MacLachlan as Jeffrey Beaumont. Opposite: Is she a murderess, a victim, or both? The haunted and haunting Vallens peers from her apartment at Jeffrey, who is pretending to be an exterminator in an attempt to solve a murder mystery. "I don't know if you're a detective or a pervert," says Laura Dern as Sandy Williams. In a film defined by moral ambiguity, he's a little bit of both.

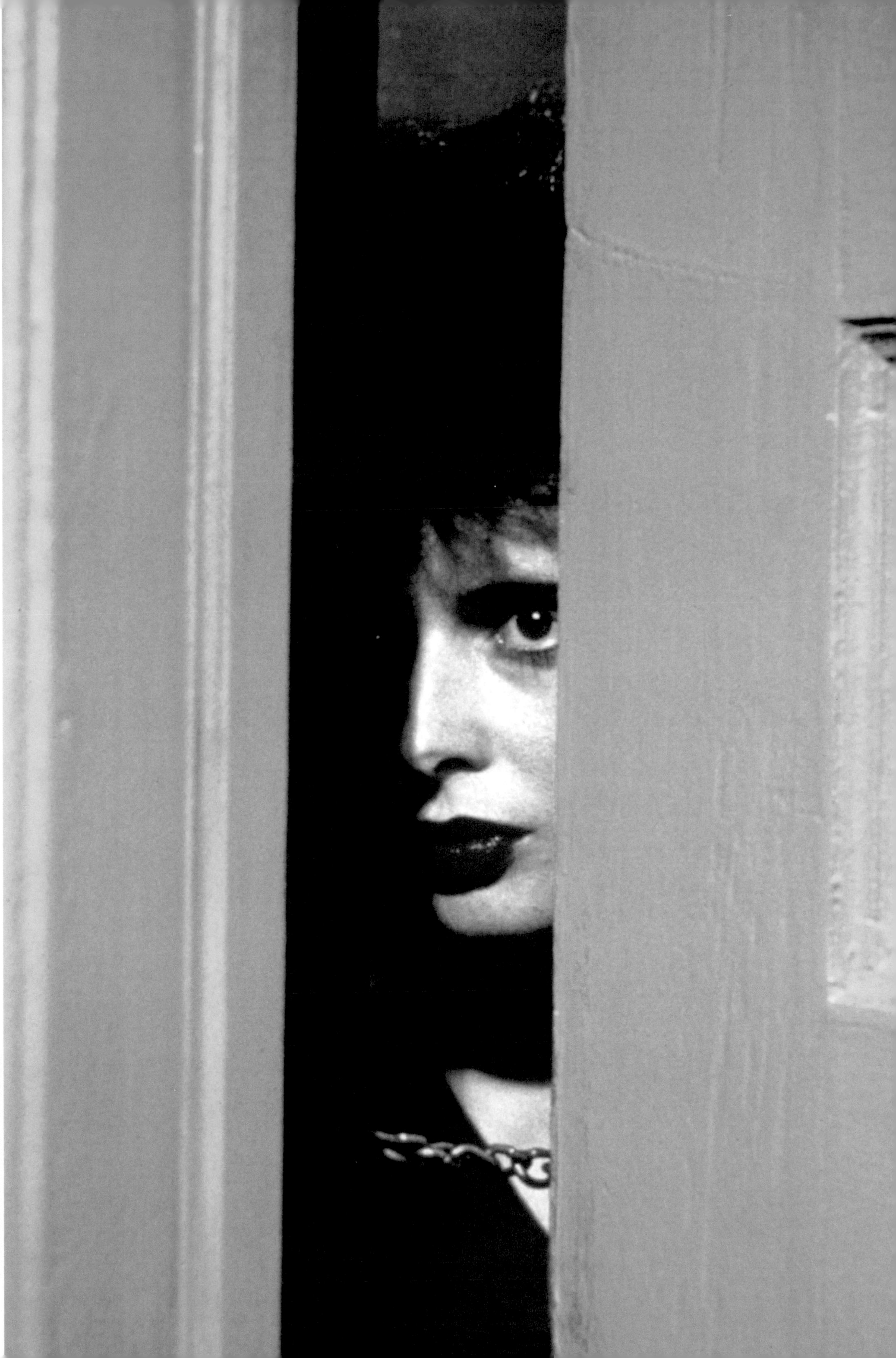

Pulp Fiction

DIR. QUENTIN TARANTINO

t was the movie no one wanted, directed by a largely unproven geek, with only one bankable star—and it ended up a box-office smash that "affected film for 20 years," David Koepp, coscreenwriter of *Jurassic Park*, tells LIFE. In fact, it fueled "nothing less than the reinvention of mainstream cinema," critic Owen Gleiberman wrote in the pages of *Entertainment Weekly*.

The film, of course, was *Pulp Fiction*, and the director was Quentin Tarantino, who not long before had been an impoverished video-store clerk in suburban Los Angeles. In 1992, he had achieved some success as the writer-director of *Reservoir Dogs*, a modestly budgeted heist film. The movie garnered significant attention and, more important, provided Tarantino the $50,000 he needed to finance a trip to Amsterdam, where he intended to pen his next project.

Inspired by a lifetime of movie-watching and a clutch of crime novels, the 30-year-old would get

Director Quentin Tarantino's trademark cartoonish approach to violence is abundantly apparent in this scene with John Travolta and Samuel L. Jackson.

RONALD GRANT/MARY EVANS/EVERETT

up, walk around the city's famed canals, "then drink like 12 cups of coffee, spending my entire morning writing," he told *Vanity Fair*. Over three months, he filled a dozen school notebooks with his jottings, resulting in a first draft that resembled, according to friend and amanuensis Linda Chen, "the diaries of a madman."

Every major studio passed on the project, and it wasn't until Bruce Willis signed on that the film had anything resembling a bankable star. But *Pulp Fiction* became a triumph, turning the detritus of American pop culture into a giddy, twisty masterpiece composed of three interlocking stories: "The ones you've seen a zillion times: the boxer who's supposed to throw a fight and doesn't, the mob guy who's supposed to take the boss's wife out for the evening, the two hit men who come and kill these guys," Tarantino said.

Reflecting both the modernist *Cahiers du Cinéma* and B-movie dreck, the film unified a series of opposites: violence and buffoonery, poetry and vulgarity, and—not least—authenticity and artifice. When actor Harvey Keitel probed the young auteur about the source of his work's street-smart qualities—had he grown up on the mean streets, in a family steeped in crime?—Tarantino answered simply: "I watch movies."

Opposite: Shall we dance? Uma Thurman and Travolta cut the rug in a film that mixed genre tropes with throw-away pop culture (Quarter Pounders, Fonzie) and giddily propulsive action—becoming, in the process, somehow greater than the sum of its parts. Above: The tyro director on the set of the film no one wanted to make. "*Every* major studio passed," producer Lawrence Bender told *Vanity Fair*. But the film went on to become a major critical and box-office hit. In the process, it resurrected the career of actor John Travolta, who was, at the time, "less than zero," according to Tarantino's agent.

L.A. Confidential

DIR. CURTIS HANSON

On December 25, 1951, seven men were severely beaten by LAPD cops after an altercation at a downtown Los Angeles bar. Known as "Bloody Christmas," the incident led to the first grand jury indictments and the first criminal convictions for the use of excessive force in the history of the LAPD. According to the municipal judge, the case "stinks to high heaven and all the perfumery in Arabia cannot obliterate its stench."

The holiday homicide helped inspire noir legend James Ellroy's 1990 novel *L.A. Confidential*, which served, in turn, as the basis for the film of the same name. Set in 1953, the story follows three LAPD officers— one by-the-book (Guy Pearce), one thuggish (Russell Crowe), and one opportunistic (Kevin Spacey) as they investigate a multiple murder at the Nite Owl café.

In the process, they discover a connection to the Fleur-de-Lis call girl network, whose prostitutes are forced to get plastic surgery to look like Hollywood starlets. They also uncover the murder of a male prostitute involved in a bribery scheme—and plenty of other corruption that, well, stinks to high heaven. The film's 1950s setting reflects "a point in time when the whole dream of Los Angeles, from that apparently golden era of the '20s and '30s, was being bulldozed," according to director Curtis Hanson.

Like much of Ellroy's work, *L.A. Confidential* is an incendiary mix of fiction and nonfiction involving Lana Turner; her violent lover, Johnny Stompanato; and then-police chief William Parker. And the film's *Hush-Hush* magazine is modeled on the real-life celebrity scandal rag *Confidential*, whose targets included Grace Kelly, Liberace, and Frank Sinatra. (Putting the *National Enquirer* to shame, the magazine called bad-boy actor Robert Mitchum "The Nude Who Came to Dinner," claiming that he took off his clothes at a party, spread ketchup on his body, and announced, "This is a masquerade party, isn't it? Well, I'm a hamburger.") But the film turns Ellroy's sprawling, sometimes self-indulgent narrative into a tight, nasty little thriller that may just make you forget all the perfumery of Arabia.

Plainclothes LAPD officers Bud White (Russell Crowe) and Ed Exley (Guy Pearce) on the beat in L.A. Confidential.

PHOTOFEST

Just One More

The great Alfred Hitchcock frames a scene on the Santa Rosa, California, set of 1943's *Shadow of a Doubt*. The film's evocative treatment of small-town life was driven, in large part, by coscreenwriter Thornton Wilder, best known for his Pulitzer Prize–winning play *Our Town*. Hitch and Wilder found a local house they thought was perfect for their filmic family, but when the owner learned that it was going to be in a movie, he had it painted. "So we had to go in and get his permission to paint it dirty again," the director said.

Made in the USA
Middletown, DE
14 June 2018